Meet Erdene

By Sue Graves

CELEBRATION PRESS
Pearson Learning Group

Contents

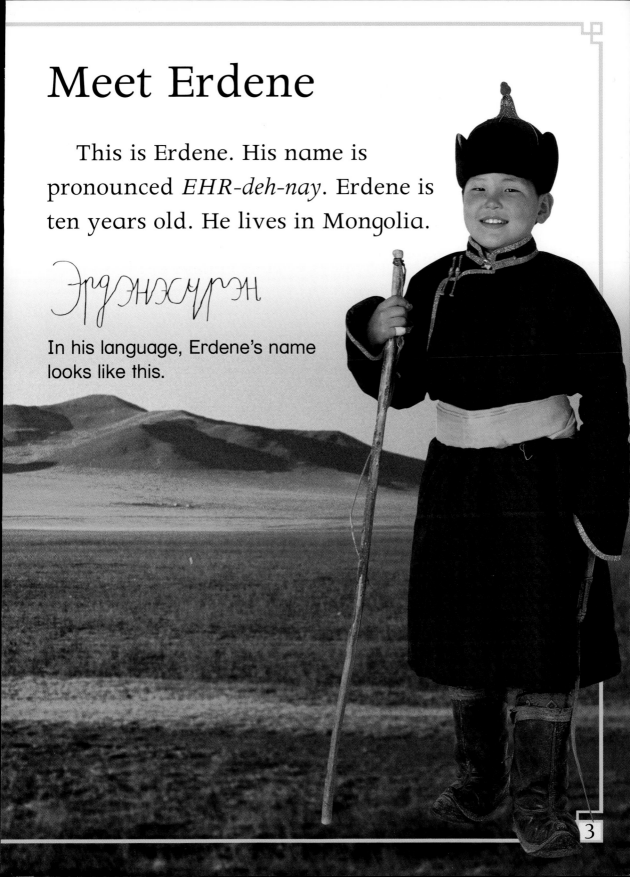

Meet Erdene

This is Erdene. His name is pronounced *EHR-deh-nay*. Erdene is ten years old. He lives in Mongolia.

Эрдэнэсүрэн

In his language, Erdene's name looks like this.

Mongolia is a country in Asia. It lies between Russia and China. Erdene and his family live in eastern Mongolia.

ASIA

Russia

Ulaanbaatar

Sergelen

Mongolia

Erdene lives here

China

Map Key

⊛ Capital city

◉ Town

— National boundary

In much of Mongolia it is cold almost all year long. There is wide, open land with grassy hills. There are few trees. Very few people live there.

Erdene lives with his parents and his older sister Oyun. He also has an older brother named Batmunkh. Batmunkh lives nearby with his wife and children.

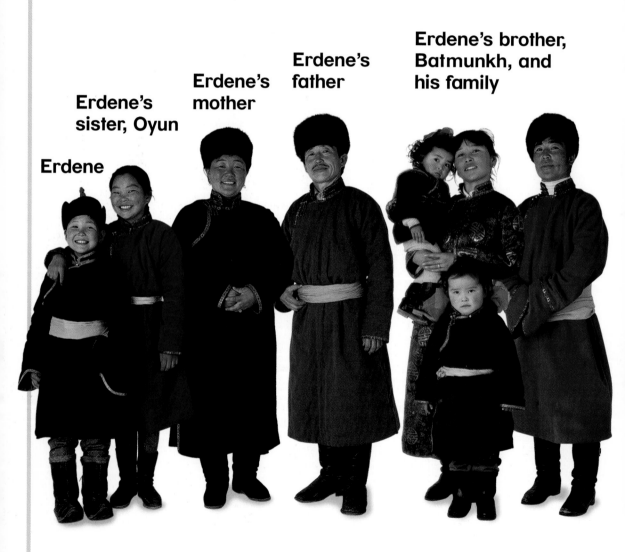

Erdene's brother, Batmunkh, and his family

Erdene's father

Erdene's mother

Erdene's sister, Oyun

Erdene

Erdene has two different homes. During the week his family lives in a house in a village called Sergelen. On weekends the family lives on a farm in a rural area about 6 miles from Sergelen. The family raises sheep, horses, cows, and goats.

Erdene lives in this house during the week.

Life During the Week

From Monday to Friday Erdene and his sister go to this school in Sergelen. Erdene likes math and reading. His favorite class is gym because he likes to run.

Like other children, Erdene studies handwriting in school. The Mongolian language has two different alphabets. Most of the time Erdene writes in the Cyrillic alphabet. He's also learning another Mongolian alphabet that was used many years ago.

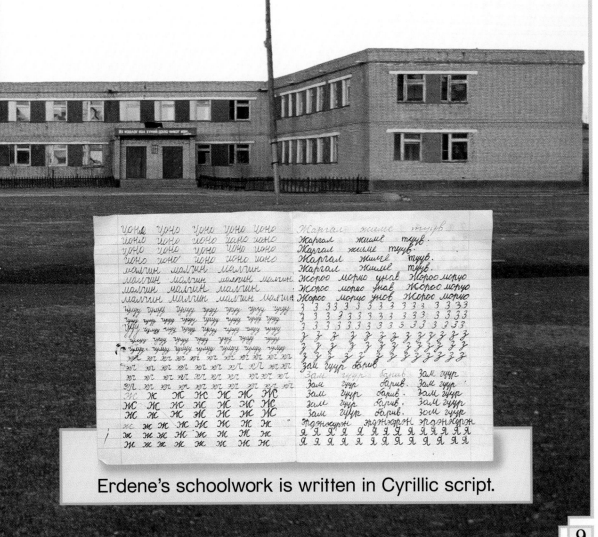

Erdene's schoolwork is written in Cyrillic script.

After school Erdene often plays outside with his friend Amraa. During the cold winter months Erdene wears a *deel* when he goes outside. Mongolians have worn this kind of coat for many years. Wool on the inside of the *deel* keeps Erdene warm.

Erdene and Amraa often play with *shagai*. These are game pieces made from the anklebones of sheep.

Erdene and Amraa wear *deels* in the winter.

Erdene

Amraa

Time for dinner! Erdene's family doesn't eat many vegetables. That's because it's hard to grow food crops in Mongolia's harsh climate. Instead the family often eats mutton. This meat comes from sheep.

Erdene's mother often makes mutton soup.

These are two of Erdene's favorite foods.

biscuits ▶

▲ mutton noodle soup

On the Weekend

On weekends Erdene and his family stay at their farm. Their home is a large, round tent. The tent is called a *ger*.

Many Mongolians live in *gers* like these.

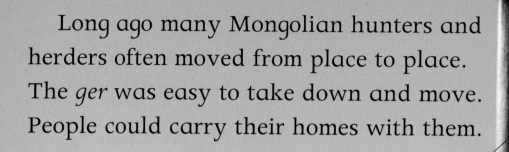

Long ago many Mongolian hunters and herders often moved from place to place. The *ger* was easy to take down and move. People could carry their homes with them.

chimney

Erdene and his family stand in front of their *ger*.   hole to let light in

The *ger* Erdene's family lives in has a wooden frame. The frame is covered with felt to keep the inside warm. The canvas on the outside of the *ger* is held in place with ropes made from horse tails.

canvas

horse-tail ropes

Inside the *ger* there's a hole in the ceiling. It lets in light. The *ger* also has a chimney that lets smoke from the stove escape.

▲ The beds in the *ger* have brightly colored rugs and cushions.

◄ The stove is used for cooking and heating the *ger*.

Inside Erdene's *ger* it is warm and cozy.

Erdene loves going to the *ger* on weekends and school vacations. He likes being outside and helping his father take care of the farm.

This is Erdene with his dog, Hoilog. He also has another dog and a horse.

Summertime Fun

During the summer Erdene helps herd his family's sheep. Many sheep live in Mongolia. They graze all year on the grassy hills.

Sometimes Erdene herds the sheep on foot. Other times he rides his horse. He makes sure the sheep stay together and don't wander off.

Once a wolf appeared when
Erdene was herding the sheep.
"I was very scared, and
I ran away," he says.

For Erdene the best part of the summer is racing his horse in the Naadam Festival. This celebration takes place every summer in Mongolia. Erdene rides in a race that is about 20 miles long. Only children are allowed to ride in the race.

Many children ride horses in the Naadam Festival.

What does Erdene want to do in the future? "When I grow up, I want to learn how to drive a car," he says. Right now, though, riding his horse will do.

Pronunciation Guide

Amraa	(ahm-RU)
Batmunkh	(but-mohnk)
Cyrillic	(sir-RIL-ik)
deel	(deel)
Erdene	(EHR-deh-nay)
ger	(gehr)
Hoilog	(HOI-luhg)
Naadam	(NAY-dam)
Oyun	(oh-YOON)
Sergelen	(seh-rehg-LEHN)
shagai	(sha-GY)